Journeying
— *selected poems*

by Wendy Mulhern

Copyright © 2013 Wendy Mulhern
All rights reserved.
ISBN: 1493774913
ISBN-13: 978-1493774913

To my mom

Contents

Introduction	9
I. Journeying	11
Hum	13
Emerging	14
Entering	15
Still Point	16
Transformation	17
El Dorado Canyon	18
What we are made of	19
Not what we thought	20
Bicycle Soliloquey	21
Development	22
What Joy Looks Like	23
The realm of light	24
Small	25
Drifting	26
All is Well	27
Chrysalis	28
Fifty Years	29
Ranging	30
Wilderness	31
Afterglow	32
Day's End	33
Temptation	34
Starlight	35
On Fire	36
Life Song	37
After the Equinox	38
Bringing it Home	39
Sinking	40
The nibbled edges of my day	41
All these things	42
Everyone Gets to Come	43
Burning	44

II. Thought's Landscapes ... 47
True Stories ... 48
Understanding ... 49
On Story ... 50
Story Problem ... 52
Thought Channels ... 53
Evening, Home ... 54
Still ... 55
A page from the biking philosopher's notebook ... 56
The shine of every day ... 57
What I'm here for ... 58
Foundational Principles ... 59
Prelude to a Dream ... 60
Perfection ... 61
Approaching the infinite ... 62
Touching Infinity ... 63
Lights ... 64
Sadness ... 65
Sand Castle ... 66
After the flood ... 67
Facebook Photos ... 68
Moving On ... 69
City Musings ... 70
An empty page ... 71
Implicate Order ... 72
If everything is made of thought ... 73
Untying Time ... 74
End of Game ... 76
And then 77

III. Earth Whispers — 79

- Rain — 81
- Bike Ride to Brackett's Landing — 82
- Summer evening grace — 83
- Night Beach — 84
- Thought Balancing — 85
- Solstice — 86
- Morning Bike Ride — 87
- True Summer — 88
- Tonight the moon — 89
- After the fireworks — 90
- August — 91
- Autumn: Three Leaves — 92
- Autumn Spinning — 93
- November — 94
- End of November — 95
- Weather Report — 96
- Imbolc — 97
- Moon Lullaby — 98
- Turning — 99
- The Dawn of Spring — 100
- Sacred Unfolding — 101
- Mid-Spring, 6:10 AM — 102
- Taste of spring — 103
- Seattle Sun — 104
- Good Night — 105
- Wet June — 106
- Summer Evening — 107
- View out the window — 108
- Stardom — 109
- Seattle Summer — 110
- Reunion — 111
- The rhythm of summer — 112
- Daily Poems — 113

IV. Prayer — 115

- Holding On — 116
- In this house of prayer — 118
- a humble prayer — 119
- One Thing — 120
- Love's Plan — 121
- Pool of Bethesda — 122
- Learning to Heal — 123
- Healing — 124
- Lullaby for Heather — 125
- Lullaby for Edward — 126
- Bedtime Prayer — 127
- Shared Prayer, King County Jail — 128
- Prayer at the End of Days — 129
- Arcturus and his sons — 130
- Light's drawing — 131
- Another prayer of thanks — 132
- Praying in the dark — 133
- Cradling Prayer — 134
- Prayer for myself — 135
- Guidance Prayer — 136
- A Moment — 137
- Peace Channel — 138
- Vision Prayer — 139
- "In my Father's house" — 140
- Fundamental frequency — 141
- Steadying — 142
- Companioned Prayer — 143
- The Light of Truth — 144
- About the author — 146
- About these poems — 146

Introduction

An introduction, at its best, should be a launching site. It could be a platform where those who feel timid about poems could reassure themselves before stepping in. Or it could be a bouncy diving board for those eager to immerse themselves. I don't want this one to keep you on the outside for too long. All these poems are journeys of some sort, though they take place in different realms. Wade in or dive in, and enjoy!

- Wendy Mulhern

I. Journeying

— travels in transformation

Hum

Words sing around my head like lullabies
Phrases rendered senseless by the light
Find meaning in the chambers of my almost
sleep. Murmurs remembered as melody
Before the mind knew they were words
Bring comfort, company and soft-hued harmony
So when I rise and look up quickly
Just in time to see a patch of blue
Ushered off hurriedly by efficient clouds
I also sense, like words that flit away as I awake
A flash of radiant possibility

Emerging

Gaze into the atmospheric eye
Until it draws you in,
Drives you through its shadows
Where the forces push you
Downward, onward,
Through the sheath of rain
Into the after-mist
To float in distant gathering of light

Choose your transformation —
Any one will do —
The dreaming earth
will softly turn
beneath her blanket
But for you
wide awake and streaming through the changes
it will be
Initiation into mystery.

Entering

Bring nothing with you,
for everything you need
is in your power to see what's here

And there's a lightness in knowing
every moment has, within it,
deep wells of richness,
plenty for your present thriving

There's no lack
of the substance in yourself
that calls forth that dark glow —
the subterranean shining
that quenches every thirst.

Still Point

Seeking stillness,
seeking coolness,
you sink gratefully
into the center point
where everything expands
in endless depth,
patterns and colors
incidental to the clear focus
as the stillness opens on and on —
round sound welcomes you in,
with ample room for echoes.
There is as much time here
as it ever takes
to coalesce, to find home,
to be reborn.

Transformation

In the chrysalis
there's nothing to talk about —
nothing of the former experience
with any relevance
to the transformation at hand

Unless, of course, there is —
unless the subtle flavors
of all those different leaves
you munched voraciously
with no articulation as to why —
Will now reveal themselves to be
precisely what you needed,
as their gifts are taken in and reconfigured
in the life for which the caterpillar had no words
but maybe somehow craved.

El Dorado Canyon

I fall into this place,
into a space deeper than words,
deeper than names and concepts,
deep as the dark pink of these boulders,
fresh fallen, broken open,
deep as the cool shadows
holding out against the cooking climb of sun,
hidden as the paths of roots
buried by rockfall,
thrusting and exploring underground
like those that twist along the surface
before they dive in.

No words can reach here now,
in the sudden knowledge
that flows along contours
and reveals itself
in cracks along the fractured face of rock
and in the eager shining path of streams
and their cold like gold
against my bare feet.

Later I will surface
and try to capture it with words,
Like that stone underside captures
light ripples from the stream,
like those dragonfly wings shine
bright against the sky.

What we are made of

The world is framed in elemental waves —
the vibrant patterns every movement follows,
the undulations rolling through the forms
of squirrels, snakes, whole flocks of birds, one swallow;
The gracious give of tree limbs in the wind,
the water's lullaby against the shore,
the ebb and flow of cricket song, the hum of bees,
reverberating ring of crystals deep in caves.
We find these very waves define our arcs:
the impulse as we launch into our stride
is carried, wave on wave, as we continue —
harmonic pattern on which we then ride . . .
How could we frame ourselves particulate
feeling these waves that all our moves articulate?

Not what we thought

We are the beings who fly
with our minds,
the ones who see the underlying patterns,
expressions of the matrix
of all the rolling powers,
everything that moves
in the stately flow
afforded by eternity,
infinitely fast or slow,
ineffable

We are the beings who find the fulcra
where the patterns turn,
and with our understanding,
we can touch them
so they bloom
into ever more involved unfoldment —
Not hemmed in by these,
the temporary forms we thought defined us,
not condemned to stumble blind
amid the powers that bind us

We are the beings who ride,
standing, reins in hand,
down the face of nature's spirals
Let us remember
We are not helpless,
not what we thought.
When we stand strong
in humbleness and service,
We're so much more.

Bicycle Soliloquey

Fog turns thought inward
while vapors collecting turn my arm hairs white
and touch my face like many small kisses.
This I want:
For all my light within to signal
from the source that it reflects,
For me to see in other mirrors
that same light my heart collects,
For it to radiate in splendor
so each mirror bearer knows
how much glory we engender,
how intense our essence glows.
I want it more than owning,
more than praise,
more than knowing
that I'm held in someone's heart
(tempting desires that always disappoint)
While being lights together
satisfies my need forever
and fulfills
hopes I never fully dare express —
Unity, collective happiness.

Development

Let rain wash around my stones,
Let wind drop fallen leaves
along my fences,
Let the gathered nutrient
from all my edges
call forth ever richer
teaming life

Build up my attention along contour
so what flows to me slows down,
Drops its gift to my receiving gratitude
Let me take the time to soak it in

There is no end
to the permission Life gives
and the ever-presence
of its care,
Its willingness to bless
gives rise to ever new recurrences
of the splendid circle
where all the living things
resound in bliss.

What Joy Looks Like

I'll tell you what
I'll tell you what joy looks like
Looks like that cloud
Stretching out its four arms
Against the blessed sky
Curling slowly inward towards itself
And reaching out again
Embracing blue

Looks like that day moon
White as the cloud
Diving down to it
Mouth wide open

I'll tell you what
I'll tell you what joy looks like
Looks like that man
Riding his bike no hands
Clapping to some tune or thought
Only he can hear

I'll tell you what joy tastes like
Tastes like this day
Leaves smelling of fall
Day full of journey and purpose
And sweet bright air.

The realm of light

Though I have thought myself
A small puddle
Look how much sky
I reflect
See these deep-limbed trees
Reaching, now naked, into subtle blue —
Dance of their branches weaving
Towards those distant clouds

Such a little patch of water
But how much brightness
Has found itself in me!
And if you look in sideways
You'll see the scene extended
beyond my edge —
Some vast inverted underworld
Suspended and inviting —
Another kingdom
In the realm of light.

Small

to meet my need to be small,
to be tiny,
minute enough to float on air currents,
light enough to not fall —
what but a being too vast to fathom?
too grand to feel anything but love.
let it fold me in
like a baby mouse
or the hatchling of a hummingbird
or a mote floating
in the infinity of its care.
let me lose
all sense of grandiosity,
all sense of power,
all sense of being something to trumpet.
it trumpets me anyway
even though I'm so small,
small as the hum of vibration
on a harp string
in awe
of having been given
my song.

Drifting

Lapping over my consciousness
like waves of incoming tides,
Cross-currents weaving
between each others phases,
The soporific influence
of three fronts:
The lateness of my sleeping
The coldness of the day
The dream-like memories
of last night's celebrating —
Doubled rhythms
concatenate along the line of waves.
So I have drifted
and the forward march of progress
has been arrested,
attention sifted,
and the beach-ward wash of thoughts
bobs there suspended
Till some renewed resolve should lift me clear
Return me to my traction on the shore.

All is Well

The circle spins around again to stillness
The wave has crested and it glides back down
In the ebb it murmurs and regathers
Readies for another go around
Even in this quiet place, there's movement
Rivulets returning to their source
Slow building for the next essential moment
When once again the cresting will burst forth
I flew! I flew, and I will fly again
Though now it feels most perfect to be still —
Give no attention to the gradual build —
When it will break, or even if it will.
All's well — in this soft place I'll trust the flow:
When it's time to leap again, I'll know.

Chrysalis

This chrysalis
is a holy state —
Intake ceased
Action halted
Identity held suspended

A time for quiet focus of awareness
The necessity for everything
that's yet unformed
The coalescence
of ideas and elements
The microscopic gravitation
of that which goes together
Furled wings, curled fingertips
Slow emerging clarity

In time you will step forth
Your power rise to meet the new demands
But while you need this firm container
this darkness, this external shielding
It will stay with you

Watch within
You'll see the signs
And you'll know when to follow
every finished impulse
into the day.

Fifty Years

A half century
isn't even half a dream cycle
for a rock
which may sit impassive
or be carried
or be dropped
where, if it's reencountered
it will be the same

But in a half century
a forest can swallow a town
that has been abandoned,
Push up trunks through old foundations,
Cover up the markers with its leaf fall

Fifty seasons, fifty rounds of rain and wind
tracked across the land,
Recorded in the memory
of tree rings, river beds
and consciousness,
Fifty years, each singular
And at once the same.

And if we rise
and travel through
a cycle of awareness,
coming back to where we see the whole,
Then fifty years is ending and beginning
A season in the journey of the soul.

Ranging

What starts as early morning bliss
may bolt—grow gangly in the climbing sun
and come to feel like hunger
and pace, in search of consummation—
Some outlet, some release
some clasp of hands
to close the circuit
and bring peace.

What soothes the ranging heart?
Is there a circle big enough
and close enough
to draw it in?
A quest for it to take
A stepping forward?
—An act of prayer
that settles it in channels
where it can deepen
as it flows down
to its sea.

Wilderness

Walking here
I have to admit
I don't know anything —
Nothing I could package
and deliver as a
Thing That I Have Learned.
I have no map for myself —
No one's words hover at my shoulder,
especially not my own —
no conclusion I can make,
no lesson I can take from here on forward.
In what way can I say I know anything,
of life, of love, of death?

Yet when I close my eyes
and follow my breath
into the undergrowth of dream,
I feel like a wilderness
and it feels good.

Afterglow

After dark
sunshine exacts its sweet toll
in currency of sleep,
each coin glinting with the memory
of sun-soaked scenes
in golds and greens,
each one heavy,
pulling my attention down
into a pool of lassitude
where all intention melts
behind the pulsing
of the heat returning to the night,
rising from my skin,
recounting every moment,
drawing me in.

Day's End

Quiet evening closes in,
Light gathers into lamplit circles,
Sky outside exudes its final magic,
Trees recede serenely into shadows.

All the ranging efforts of the day return,
Pool their energy into the center,
Strong internal processors now softly burn,
assimilating what the day has meant

Each time of holding up the light
has played its part,
Each act of empathy
imprinted in your heart
will bring its fruits
in surer shining of the truth
to satisfy your soul and bring rebirth
and serve as affirmation of your worth.

Temptation

The surf of sleep waits just behind my eyes,
It hushes, rushes, and recedes,
It drags, like shells,
my focus and resolve,
It tugs them under, covers them
and smiles.
It whispers at me as I move
from task to task, a little dazed
by water's movement,
crossways
to where I try to walk.
It murmurs: it's preparing
a big wave to bring me down with it.
Succumb, it soothes, come down
to where the dreams can slosh against your side
and wash you, cuddle you, caress your hair
I'm thinking soon
I may surrender —
. . . almost there . . . .

Starlight

There is no existential fact of night —
the word speaks of the endless depth of space,
the field wherein the play of stars is staged —
Each star gives tribute to the light.

Each star must serve the existential light,
the pulse within, essential churning force
which rises out of need and tumbles forth —
We see their sharp travail across the night.

We see their offering across the night
and know we, too, must ever do the same —
we too must birth our inner urgent flame —
Each life gives tribute to the light.

On Fire

Throw another log into the furnace
Pump the bellows, let the heat keep rising
For, whether on purpose or by chance
It seems I am committed —
Open to alloys,
Open to alchemy,
Whatever will meld,
Whatever may emerge,
That which will grow stronger
as it melts and flows together,
That which will arise transformed
to something unimagined.
Though the steams arise and cloud my sight,
Creative sparks in circling outward flight
will forge a more expansive view,
herald the birth of something new,
While anything that's burning off,
consigned to ash, will float away
without my even noticing:
The fire is where I am today.

Life Song

Let me inhabit
the song that I am,
Let its melody course
through my limbs,
Let the deep crystal harmony
roll out its hum in me
Filling my center with bliss

With the trace taste of
dust of the high mountain rocks
washed in the snowmelt,
cleansed in its rushing fall
Telling the story
of timeless eternity,
Sending the rhythm on down,
And the soft scent of blossoms
So light and ephemeral —
Subtle insistence on living in now

Let me inhabit
the song that I am,
Learn from my heart and my bones
How I have known this for thousands of years,
How I now come to my own.

After the Equinox

You step from summer's warm embrace
to meet the arms of fall —
impassioned lover
seizing you with fervent grasp,
taking your breath away —
bright promises withdrawn and offered many times,
driven rain between the shafts of sun,
sweeping you along toward deep adventure

So fall demands that you be new
It calls you to pull forth deep resources
from your inner being
for travel into mystery.
It offers you no guarantee
of warmth or soft security,
Instead it summons acts of daring
invigorating rigor, fortitude
Calling you to prove, with deeds, your caring
Teaching you a deeper gratitude.

Bringing it Home
(for Edward)

I ride into the bright sunshine,
Push against the strong wind,
Glide within the soothing shade that lets me see.
And I am loved by all of these,
And by the sweet air
And by the soft seas —
I bring the love of all these lovers
Home to you.
You'll see it in my eyes
And smell it in my skin and hair,
You'll take me in your arms
And they will be there
And they will make you want them
As they make you want me,
We all will flow together
As it should be.
So with my many lovers
I am still true —
Enriched to be with them
And bring it home to you.

Sinking

The water closes over it
and it's gone,
The ripples lap over each other
and disappear —
no sign left that anything
was ever here.
Other perturbations take their turn.
The water takes its color from the sky.
The sky is deep; within it, many echoes.
Across its breadth, a varied palette stretches.
The water's depth may thus stay undefined —
how far, how deep, how slow, how wandering
may be the drop down to the ocean's floor.
The surface stillness leaves a space for pondering
what worlds beneath have slipped away before,
and if the momentary ease of foundering
should be resisted. Help me find the shore.

The nibbled edges of my day

The native flute invokes a woodland scene —
soft-warbled water, sifting sun through trees —
high descant; low, soothing melodies
that move me subtly halfway into dream.
The sounds around me lull me into trance,
the scenes to illustrate them build
behind my eyes, rise up with crafty skill
and bend the sounds to orchestrate their sense.
Which one came first? Before I know, I'm gone —
the train of thought my will suggested — flown —
Too brief for dream, the images all turn
like pages, sound and sight and touch as one.
Fine workmanship - in fairy dust they're drawn —
They take away my hours at night and dawn.

All these things

All these things
await the touch of your eyes,
their molecules mirrors
to show you what you are.
The soft humility
which lets you receive
each stone, each dewdrop
and all the myriad leaves
which you have said you loved
cannot be lost to you.
Practice helps
and if you can silence the chatter
it helps. No worry—
All these things
still wait for you.
No hurry —
You have eternity to reciprocate
their touch.

Everyone Gets to Come

Don't be afraid —
Don't look ahead in dread
of narrowing life choices,
of chances missed.
It doesn't matter —
for in the plan of days,
Everyone gets to come.

To the grand reception
of our timeless gifts,
to the celebration
of what we've always been,
to the home that holds us
splendid and beloved,
Everyone gets to come.

In the great rapture
of interaction in the moment,
in that enchanting weightlessness
where you can't tell for sure
if the impulse comes from you
or from another
(though it is yours as surely as you feel it)
In the joy of that transporting,
far beyond what you could know to ask for,
Everyone gets to come.

Burning

And every door you go through,
you leave behind another thing
Whole worlds forgotten like dreams —
Only emotions, trailing in threads,
remain, remind you something . . .
And then they're gone
And you're still moving
And you're still here
While everything you thought you were
dissolves
And in the tingle
You may think you're fading too
But here you are
Still moving forward
Burning through
A comet on a wide elliptic arc
Your changes - blazing gifts
against the dark.

II.
Thought's Landscapes
— stories, dreams, explorations

True Stories

No story is the truth
but there are true stories.
If story is the arc on which you fly,
some will launch you clean and true,
and where you sail
will be the place you feel
the rising up of what you are
to meet the opportunity,
the awesome, scary challenge
calling forth your deep integrity.

A story that is true
will keep on ringing
with fractal echos still reverberating,
the rightness of the patterns it's creating
affirming you,
forever reinstating
what you have always been
and now shall be:
A story that is true
will set you free.

Understanding

Turn the tumblers, one and then another —
For you to enter, all must be aligned —
It opens to the easy spinning
of your secret
Or to the deep discernment
of a listening mind.

Don't settle for the superficial level,
The one that opens up without a key,
Where all may stroll
but none may know the meaning;
For to be true, the entrance must be deep.

Beneath the layer of rationalization,
Beneath the tallies of the service due,
Beneath self-image and self-fabrication,
A more fulfilling essence waits for you.

Go deep, for underneath
the thoughts that you can voice as words,
You'll feel the breath and pause
whose choice is to be heard
in silence, and in limpid images
that let you understand what really is.

On Story

I.

Although I know
that story is a tool
with which to carve
the potent wave of feelings
and stir and move emotions
along the course the story indicates,
Today
Let me not try
to carve them,
Let me not define
with story
what it is I feel,
Let the weather go through me —
the rain,
the strong wind,
that which beats against
the inside of my eyes,
And let me be
like a field
that takes in rain,
lets it spread deep into the roots,
Compels the sudden bloom
of countless flowers.

II.

I once said,
to be without a story
is to be without a home
and you have to go and live
in someone else's story,
a supporting character
who sleeps on their couch
and drinks their leftover coffee
before they wake up —
brown ring on the cup —
no choice of your own.
but now I see
To live without a story
is to live
on the edge that is always unfolding
with new surprises —
A tale you've never heard before.

Story Problem

Here is a place of feeling lonely,
a point of discontinuity,
a no man's land between the asymptotes —
X marks the degenerate set.
No bounding parabolic curve for me,
 — ever upward, ever steeper —
no perfect circle, no elegant ellipse,
no connection to the conic section.

Here is a place of feeling lonely,
a point of discontinuity,
no connection to logic or reality
or the events of the day.
Can I fall, thus
down along the asymptotes,
ever approaching,
never fully touched?

Thought Channels

Thought's landscape — how it changes,
    how the current rearranges,
        deepens here, deposits there,
            accenting flows, directing rivulets —
Thought follows patterns
    in its swift recursions,
        pushing at the rock,
            wearing deeper channels.
    As it flows swifter
      it may push
         over formerly dry edges,
            trip itself, dislodging stones,
      fall into a new course
which then in mounting rushes
    it can follow
        And the force of it
           occasions new attention
                And the joy of it
                    invokes a new dimension
            And the pulse of it
      thunders the perfection
of another way to think and feel —
    another thing
        now known as real.

Evening, Home

Well, I won't dwell on
the little unravellings at the edges —
backwash of doubts about an interaction,
nagging thoughts of having done it wrong —

Better to remember
the afternoon light
and the touch of hands
with the home-soaring
but ever unexpected joy
that flew like swallows
from the moment of connection,

Better to notice
how deep and ultimately unerring
is the impulse
that stands behind me
ready to pour out
from my eyes and mouth and fingertips
when I am attentive,
when I give consent.

Still

In the absence of words
the mind still does its melodies,
sometimes with attention,
sometimes not,
and images may rise to meet the tunes

In the absence of conscious thought
the breath of life can still entrance —
so many variations to its inrush,
so many swirls within the currents
of its outward flow

In the absence of direction
the heart's impulse, still present,
guides the mind into the stillness
before the words —
the quiet spring,
the soft upwelling
of what most needs to be heard.

A page from the biking philosopher's notebook
- for Jennifer

As it is written
in the paws of a dog,
in the sudden life arc of a spider,
Things come to being out of thought:
From the imperative of their intent
they come to life,
stretch forth in being what they are,
without a thought of being something else,
And everything about them—form and function
(as paws that twitch and dream of running, digging)
enacts that impulse which has brought them forth
and brings them forth again in every moment.

In the ephemera we call this life
Where things and plans dissolve so fast
like dreams,
Some thought that runs
much deeper than our conscious mind
calls forth a force
more steadfast than it seems,
that orients our being to its course,
aligns our lives with our desires
and pulses us through underlying pattern —
our hands, our thoughts, and everything we are.

The shine of every day

Consider this: the shine of every day,
whether a glimmer, thin and filtered ray,
or the mute glow of pearl grey under clouds,
or bold eye-squinting light that visually shouts,
Whether a slender reed that barely bears you up,
or bubbles deep within that rocket skyward,
decorous pleasure or a vaulting joy
where you're not sure how you keep going higher,
It all expresses something you must know,
though in the rush of duties you may well forget —
A presence in your life that always shows
you're not alone, your need is always met.
Does God exist? - It doesn't matter what you say,
Just that you see the shine of every day.

What I'm here for

I have these eyes —
this intersection of perception,
this way of seeing

I have this truth at my core
that gives me context
to interpret what is here,
to understand the law
that flows in everything

I have this love
(not made by me
but found in me, as me)
It is my life to be it,
to insist that it illumine
all that I behold,
so bearing witness
with my eyes, my truth, my love
to what I am,
to what we are.

Foundational Principles

My life depends
on my getting this right.
Not as in
I'll die if I don't
so much as that
I'll live when I do,
really live.

Which means that life itself
will thrive around me
and give me life
just as I give to it,
And I will move within the brightness
of the being that fulfills me —
brings out my essence
as I bring it forth.

It is given
that I'll get it right,
If not in every case,
at least in moments,
which then must grow
till they're the only kind —
the bracing breath
on which my life depends.

Prelude to a Dream

Here is the color of the depth of Mind:
Not quite black - a greyish, bluish cast,
The place each soul has always hoped to find —
Everything said from here stands; its word will last.
Mountains are moved, all rivers speak it,
Northern lights' swift shimmer shines it past.
This is the place where nothing stands beneath it —
No cave so deep, no shifting sea so vast,
Here in the backdrop of the depth of Mind:
All secrets are spelled out, their golden stamp
is illustrated, block by block, line by line,
Impressed with every sacred word's recap.
Or so it seemed, as earnest dream descended
Submerging me in sleep before it ended.

Perfection

Some things are perfect —
delightful in every way —
nothing contrary
has any say.
Some things you win
applying
meticulous design,
Some things come so simple
they arrest your mind.
You ponder
How could this have happened?
Can I make it work again?
But you don't know the answer
so the mystery remains.
And some things, by their nature,
when you let them be,
will always come up shining
and you just may see
There's a wisdom in releasing
all your dreams to find their homes,
There's a magic in allowing things
to come into their own.

Approaching the infinite

Approaching the infinite
Some will chant, some will sing
Some will pray
Some will cry
Some will dance, naked
Some will robe themselves
in flowers and angel's wings
Some will study, some will read books
Some will build structures
Some will tend crops
Some will climb, some will run
Some will champion others
All will give everything
For only everything is enough.

Touching Infinity

With my mind
I touched infinity —
felt the satisfying curling
up and through me as smoke curls
and tendrils of vines curl
around their desired supports,
pulling them close.
I touched infinity and felt
the deep breath of relief,
two up and one long ride down,
as babies breathe when they finally
let go and slide into sleep,
felt myself flow into the wide reaches of thought,
unlimited, uncharted—the excitement and delight
of exploration, as all dimensions
open out at once.
The weightlessness
of how I travel there
a promise:
You can return here
anytime.
With my mind
I touched infinity,
a place I've been before
(magical dreams)
but didn't know
was right here.

Lights

In the dark cave of decrepit stories
we may huddle around the candle flames
of our love for each other —
a candle here, a candle there,
carefully tended or carelessly snuffed out.
We may wander,
looking for another,
another light,
another one to light our candle.
But if a chink of sky should show
through some surprising cleft of cave,
If it should shine on you or me,
I might see you transfigured
by amazing light —
Not just the small circle of your face
but all of you lit up,
and I would want you.
Or you might see me thus
and want my light
and we might cling to one another.
But wait —
Let's climb together,
Let's find others,
Make a pyramid —
Let's climb out.

Sadness

Sadness is the need to close a loop —
Something needing to be given,
Something not received,
An uncompleted sequence
Brought up short.

Your yearning runs
Along the broken circle,
Time and again arrested by the gap.
It throws its spark in stark desire,
Attempts to arc across the emptiness.

It tries, it waits, it paces, tries again,
It falls back in exhaustion, gathers strength,
You send it till it leaps across
And reaches the exalting joy
Or till you give up on the trial
And turn away.

Sand Castle

Look how it falls —
Ponderous,
turning and sinking,
its shapes tipping at wild angles
before dissolving —
its fall as inevitable
as its standing seemed to be.
No loftiness of spires
escapes the sliding from beneath
as sand surrenders to the slip of water.
No damp cohesion remains —
each grain in its communion
with the overwhelming water,
suspended, so released
from past alliances.
So little shift of tide it takes
to wash away the structure
and its memory
and leave a shining mirror
on the shore.

After the flood

Don't have much to say —
I must sit and wait
till my internal waters settle down.
The turbid sediment, roiled up
from stream beds used to quiet flow
from banks above where waters mostly run
must make its way
as far as it must go
till it can clear.

Then I'll see
just how the course has changed,
What views will stay the same,
What places where my thoughts and hopes once dwelt
will be no longer fed
and so dry out,
What unexpected new course I might find
of love to feed and occupy my mind.

Facebook Photos

What is this urge? This longing to be seen?
The double image
— being you
and watching yourself be —
Adds desperate extra light
to the edge of your intent.
If you are seen to be beloved,
perhaps you are.
The photo, captured and broadcast
is proof,
And if you're in enough of them,
you're safe —
You won't be fading out of view
until tomorrow.

Moving On

In weary sameness once again you slide your tray
past each seductive offering in the display
of nothing that could satisfy the gap within —
your plate still empty as you reach the end.
So is this why we choose to die - we lack
the bright desire to keep us coming back?
We could go on, but wonder what's the use
(the reasons, glorious before, now seem obtuse)
Or is there more than what is offered here,
a way to focus thought between the things,
to listen with a more celestial ear
for strains beyond what the commercials sing?
Seek substance in a different kind of sphere
and find the joy that strong connection brings.

City Musings

I walked, entreating the collective mind:
Look, who you are is not defined
by what you buy, or tastes refined
through careful choice of things designed
to show your status and proclaim
alignment with some product's name.

I stepped into the crosswalk, feeling wise
to turn from all the billboards for the prize
of seeing how much better we are known
for what we've striven for, what we have honed
through stretching into what the day demands,
through what we make with our own hands.

I liked my words - I thought they would compel,
except I didn't know who I could tell.

An empty page

Perhaps it is a time for breathing in,
Breathing in, taking in,
Listening instead of saying,
Having nothing to convey,
Ingesting rather than creating,
Letting rushing showers of stories
fall across my vision,
Hearing all the sounds
and making no decision.
Let the magic coalesce at other sources,
Let the message be sent out
by other voices.
This yawning blankness of my mind
may well be for the best —
Every field, including mine,
must have its time of rest.

Implicate Order

Every hidden thing
will find its way to surface
in the folding and refolding
of the necessary permutations.

All the patterns possible in each design
must lay their sequences
along the dance of time.
It isn't destiny unrolling
in a rigid line —
It's more the complex undulations of a plane
wherein no signal, however small, is lost.
Though it may seem confused, distorted, tossed
by all the other waves that intersect,
Each thing that is
will have its full effect.

If everything is made of thought

If everything is made of thought
Then there are no separate things —
No rolly, clunky, cluttery things,
No inscrutable, intractable things,
Nothing to fall out of place,
Nothing to fail to move.

If everything is made of thought
Then there is no past, no gaping track
where things tore through the fabric
of our hopes and plans,
leaving shreds along the course of time,
No regrets and no alarm,
No irreparable harm.

If everything is made of thought
Then all these things
we think are non-negotiable —
the way things are, the way they have to be —
can really change, in any instant —
Blink of an eye, awakening from dream.

Untying Time

We find ourselves as characters,
unfinished, emerging
as on time's great loom
we're woven,
The colors of our purpose and desires
slow-forming on its tapestry of story,
with wefts that wrap and then dip down
unseen,
and poke up further on between the warps —
The things we know, then don't,
then know again,
The breathless trailing edges
of our hopes . . .

But then
We may view time as our dimension,
Something we've stretched out
upon a frame,
Coordinates established by our mind force
to help us understand our vital being.

And maybe time, and time's whole tapestry
We'll take up one day, like a mighty cloak
to wrap ourselves,
But then to fling away
So we may stride in freedom
since we know
That we endure, outside of time, eternal,
And the day,
no longer bound,
may then be redefined,
And time be understood again
as rhythm,
a beat to dance, a riff to sing,
a harmony,
an endless field and we the masters,
untied from time
aloft on Spirit's wing.

End of Game

All ye all ye in free!
So we were called home
at the edge of dusk
when the lights were starting to glow
in the houses,
and the evening's cool
was softening the sky
and we would all return
to the separate circles
of those lights, and our families.

Well, it's getting to be
the end of the game
and all the chosen roles
and all the tokens
are swirling down the vortex
towards their fall —
What will we hear of next?
It's a strange thought
that everything might be falling
We can't feel it
any more than we feel the earth's spin,
But there are signs
that the whole game is ending,
so we are looking up,
ready to be called home.

And then . . .

When the whole story falls away,
sloughed off
like the great side of a glacier,
tumbling down with crashing echoes,
the silence that arises afterwards
will hold a clear and crystal space
in which the warble of a bird
will thrill,
and in the faint glacial dust
that keeps dispersing,
some very fresh taste to the air —
and our eyes
will soften
and we'll see a new light
in all the faces
and in every dewdrop
and in every life.

III. Earth Whispers
— *weather and seasons of Earth and Spirit*

Rain

It rains, it rains,
The rivulets run down
irregular but constant,
and the sound
is soporific and insistent.
That crow outside
is definitely wet —
This afternoon will grant no respite,
So I need to think
of inner light
and two delightful people
who were suns for me today,
lighting up the rooms
and spreading warmth.
The glow has stayed —
a lavished layer of brightness
in the lining of my being,
Soft as fur
Warm as tended fire.

Bike Ride to Brackett's Landing
Sunny, 60 degrees

A wind that buffets me but isn't cold,
One inhale's gift of blossom as I fly,
The sun's light touch that raises up my soul,
The water's glint as I go swiftly by,
The pattern of the shadows on the concrete,
Rails and steps on ramp up from the underpass,
The echo of my song, sustained though incomplete,
hurled down the tunnel while I'm rolling fast —
These, with the words that follow melody,
Trying their rhythms on the mellow tune
that floats within me, answering my tunnel cry,
bring heightened pleasure to my afternoon.
Ah, spring! How clear the vision you inspire!
How rich the scents! How sweet the homage you require.

Summer evening grace

As I ride homeward,
The sun begins its descent
through congregations of clouds.
They reach out to be transfigured
fleetingly, each in turn,
While the blessing flows
fleecy hand to fleecy hand.
The air is cooler,
the evening shadows softened,
the pavement glow subdued.
Later the sun reemerges —
Commanding countenance
too strong to behold.
I ride dazed, half blinded
till I slip into the shadow of a hill.

Night Beach

In the time after the sparkles
when the dark waves speak
in their low tones
along the dark beach
and the liquid heat
has drained out of the day,
Lean in close
to take in what they have to say.
Here in the hush
of night high tide
where water meets the soft sand
and the seaweeds glide,
in the last glowing of the evening sky
The ancient secrets whisper once again.
No, you will not put words on this
even though you'll hear and understand —
The soothing language of the bay
can comfort you
beyond all reason, or anything you planned.
The circle, circle, rock and rush,
persistent, peaceful, patient —
when you've gone home, this hush, recalled
will bring you here again.

Thought Balancing

Summer solstice:
We are called
to try to make something meaningful
of this blip in time,
But stones laugh
like water tripping down them
and piles of stones fall
with no propriety,
like clowns rolling,
who know how to fall
by giving and giving
and not standing on ceremony
but letting their inner dignity
fall with them like water
so it stays within,
growing stronger
as they sink to their source.
And all my efforts can fall
apart
ignominiously
like bits of fluff in the wind,
but that which centers me
will draw everything back
to its compelling core.

Solstice

Like a miracle
The celebrated day rose up, spreading its gifts —
Bird song long before we truly woke,
Then sky embracing early morning trees
with luminous touch of mackerel clouds,
Then a stretching space of blue,
desperate for warmth,
yearned towards the cloud-clamored sun.
Later, the day brought out summer
like a father returning home after too long —
In my gratitude I forget my suspicion that
he will not stay.
I drink the scent of wild roses, sun-warmed,
rejoice in wind on my arms.
A long bike ride
and work to do outside
and family differences to take in stride
as we tumble to the end
too tired to attend to any more
(A meeting took a bite out of my evening
as if it were any day . . .)

Morning Bike Ride

I can be satisfied
with this ride,
though the bends of the river tempted me
(Further down the trail, where the reflected riverbanks
braid back and forth against the river's turns,
their dance created
by the parallax
of my gliding bike,
I, thus among them,
swooping bright along their smooth dips
and the uncanny depth of sky)
I can stop here
where ducks kaleidoscope
the mirror of the placid water.
Gentle turbulence, further on,
makes the reflection perfect,
renders it in interlocking diamonds
gliding smoothly down.
Colors shimmer, dazzle —
Fireweed and roses
shine forth audacious purple and pinks,
Willow limbs thrill in reflected ripple light,
Precise lines of houses intersect the ripples' circles.
Though traffic-roar and sirens pierce the day,
The mellow quiet hovers close.
I can be satisfied
with this ride.

True Summer

These are the sounds of summer night
Served up in velvet warmth:
The braided rise and fall of cricket song, cicadas,
The murmur of the wind, and water rolling,
A clink of masts, a roar of distant traffic,
The chatter of an isolated bird.

This is the feel of summer night —
So full —
My heart as sensitized as surface skin,
A welling up of some sweet inner yearning —
Awakened pull of tides within.

Tonight the moon

Tonight the moon
Rules the waters from the east —
Royal pathway spread from shore to shore,
While to the west
The clouds with heads like trees
Or bears
Nod and whisper to each other,
Surveying the approaching dark.

After the fireworks

after the fireworks
the stars,
deeply dimensioned, nearer and farther,
great swath of milky way,
singing like crickets.

mirroring stars,
phosphorescence
erupting like fireworks
rippling and glowing,
defining our fingers and arms.

after the yes
its rewards:
a treasure to witness this
sparkling and splashing bliss,
making us wish
our beloveds were there with us,
wanting to share how we lit up the water
and how this bright night
lit us up.

August

Summer rests light upon my skin
lending ease to all my moments.
Soft skies with subtle drama
float above the day.
Evening falls mellow,
cooling breeze meanders through the house —
A brief time of timelessness
that casts its blessing
along the season's sloping curve towards fall.

Autumn: Three Leaves

I

The smile of fall —
A rare and fleeting gift
like that of one whose visage
is reflexively severe
from discipline built up through years
of self-constraint, of striving for the prize,
the burnished glow of mastery
that shines through fruit and crimson leaf
against impassioned skies.

II

But no,
for fall speaks of the grace of letting go,
the end of effort and the floating backward,
tumbled down, but glinting brilliant,
not because of winning
but for all the steady time beneath the sun,
falling as a blanket to the earth
now that the kiss of summer's done.

III

in every Autumn day
three faces —
one for looking forward,
one for looking back,
one for looking inward
toward what glows against the lack —
When green retreats,
the inner fire
will find its core
and flame up higher.

Autumn Spinning

whirling in a balance
like a maple seed descending
in late afternoon of year
as the earth keeps rolling, bending
the low arc of light more inward
in the grasp of shadows falling
as the lively air invites us
to the dance of bright leaves flaming,
so the inward hearth light calls us
to its quiet steady warmth
and the potent stillness pulls us
to its radiating strength.
so balanced - spinning outward,
folding inward,
we revolve,
strength offsetting strength,
love inspiring love.

November

We are not hardened yet for winter
Though it is November
And trees stand almost bare,
And though each day is noticeably shorter.
The frost on roofs this morning
met us unprepared —
Our bones felt cold,
our flesh tensed up against them.

We are not hardened yet for winter
Though it's not as cold as it will get.
We have the heat turned up
inside our cozy house
And we turn back like cats
when we go out.
No saunters on the sand today —
A brisk walk is required,
And even short forays outside
have left us tired.

We are not hardened yet for winter
But soon
we'll open up our doors to what it gives,
Feel the brisk cleansing of its mountain breath
that, summoning our inner fires,
calls us to live.

End of November

the birch leaves save their exit till the end,
after the flamboyant reds of maples, flame bush, plum
and the quiet fall of cherry, apple, ash,
so they can display their spray of gold
against the dark of evergreens and bare branches
and twinkle like coins as they blow in the wind,
whirl free
and settle on the ground.

Weather Report

February cold, implacable,
Seeps through around the windows and the doors;
Sun's gleam like steel, a dull and frigid glow,
Resounds in hollow tremors through my bones.
But sunrise, dawning pink, proffered a peace,
And later sunshine, almost generous,
Sent temperature to forty-five degrees,
Gave reassurance to intrepid bulbs.
Yes, light returns, it spreads over the hollows
Where puddles lay before, and sometimes ice.
Too thin for spring, but soon that too will follow,
The buds will bulge, new life's quick heat will rise.
For now, soft clouds will swaddle up the night
To ease our gentle turning towards the light.

Imbolc

Still water of the winter river
Deep moving but surface smooth
Clear reflection with a subtle shimmer
Brown, bare trees thrust into blue
Moon ghost floating in a cloudless sky
Sailing low, so pale, alone
Bikes and skaters glide on by
Through air that's soft and warm — sun owned
Its scent enticing us to dream, to yearn:
A day to celebrate the light's return.

Moon Lullaby

Lay my head on moon-touched clouds,
Suffuse my sleep with moonbeams,
Let their coolness flow along my breath,
Their sweetness reaching deep into my dreams.
So permeating, let its light refresh,
with gentle steadfastness,
my halting meditation.
Bring to me the comprehensive rest
that stills my heart's incessant perturbations.
Hold me in your light
till morning's wings arise
to bear me into day's resplendent skies.

Turning

In these times when light is mostly shrouded
(rain and fog and thick, low-lurking clouds)
We see no change, no movement of the seasons,
No shadows marking progress on the dial

Till, on a day like this
Where some incalculable hand
has parted all the shrouds, so we can see
the sun, serene, in clear, surreal cerulean,
And every limb, love-touched, in basking gleam,

And know our land is turning toward the springtime,
Her face receiving now, in every day,
A bit more light, more ease,
More time to stretch out
In life-embracing welcome —
Warm against the longer glowing sky.

The Dawn of Spring

The trees arose before the dawn of spring,
the running of their sap waking them up,
pulsing invisible and potent
underneath their bark,
inciting buds to swell.

And now their scent,
sent delicate through branch and blossom,
has touched the air with some delicious summons
to wake me up
the way the sap aroused the trees,
aliveness pumping through my piqued awareness.

Ah Spring! Such gratitude you raise
as you invoke this nameless joy
that fills my days.

Sacred Unfolding

Around a seed of thought,
substance gathers —
The infant leaf
forms itself
from nothing
and the essence of everything —
water from the network of the soil,
last year's sun released from secret storage,
love that calls them to the service
of the timeless pattern.

It forms itself
pleated, furled, or crumpled
in its tiny space.
Its weightless impulse summons energy,
more than it can hold within its sphere,
so it expands,
unfolds, unfurls, stretches out
to raise its tender head
and join the dance of spring.

Mid-Spring, 6:10 AM

After I waved good bye,
the sweet half moon
still glowed
above a soft pink cloud,
still dark
in pre-dawn's hush.

A little later
the robin started.

Taste of spring

Days like this,
I remember
how the sun can come for me —
How, even if I face it from a place of stress,
numb to any radiance or peace,
its shining will start to reach through —
Soft warming on my face,
dazzle of water sparkles on my eyes,
subtly winning ground in my attentions
till I am undone,
abandon all preoccupations
and stretch, catlike,
into the luxury of its gift.

Seattle Sun

The sun comes out
just in the evening
and it is like
giddy laughter after many tears
where you can feel your breathing
like a big drama,
now the storm has cleared,
though there's no guarantee
the flood will not return
on the flash of some re-tripped remembrance.

The sun has come
too late to warm the earth,
but old, tall trees
shake their shaggy limbs
in deep enjoyment
and send their glow
back through
my no longer spattered windows.

Good Night

Sweet bright day
draws to its close,
Companionable shadows
bring me in
to intimacy's secret sentences.
The moon that tracked
across the daytime sky
now sleeps, and leaves the cool night
to the stars

Inside the house, the ticking clocks
prepare to stand their vigil.
The noises of the day retreat
to leave them looming.
It's my time to surrender
so that dreams can have their sway
as we ride swiftly
through the curve of night
and on toward day.

Wet June

I will compose a song
in the tune of June
while the dark clouds
let light in at the distant edges
and four red lilies and one campanula
have opened in the rain
and a squirrel
chomps almost-ripe cherries
shaking raindrops from the branches
Wet June
cloaking the length of days
so close to solstice
summer so far away.

Summer Evening

Clouds on pilgrimage
seeking the convocation of thunderstorm
drift entranced,
kissed in soft pink light,
calling forth divinity of sky.

They let the current take them,
slow and meaningful
toward their unseen goal.
Sculpted pink on luminescent blue
transitions into grey on lighter grey
and on into white
against the deepened dark.

View out the window
— *Maxwelton Aerie, July 3, 2012*

The urgency of growth
captured in a gesture
of kiwi vines reaching —
a faint dusting of red
along the underside of a leaf,
light shining through it,
Given voice by the songbirds,
intimate and plentiful,
Celebrated by a wild profusion
of high-climbing roses
in shades of orange and yellow.
More flowers as you scan —
fireworks in hot pink,
poppies in peach,
Pastures beyond
darkened and illuminated in patches
by dramatic skies.
Everything is rising up
in the dance of sun and rain.

Stardom

The sun came out at six pm,
Grand, sporting brilliant blue sky
And a few gratuitous fluffy clouds —
A fine entrance —
escorted by strong winds officiously
brushing away the excess warmth.
But it was charming enough
to warm us anyway,
Make us sit and bask
if only for a moment.

It is a busy star
with many others it must see —
We can't expect its glow to last for very long
and so we try not to depend on it,
try not to hang on its every gesture.
But face it:
We are smitten —
We will pine for it tomorrow
if it's gone.

Seattle Summer

There may not be a way to find a reason
why these delicious days are rationed —
Whether to preserve their fragile, fragrant freshness
or the eagerness with which our skin receives them,
Or whether it's designed to keep us guessing,
Or ready us for some exquisite blessing
in some other realm. No matter —

The brilliance of today
will leave a mark across the summer,
Shine its golden rays
over many cloudy cold ones,
Teach us to embrace
this day, and every potent sign
of imminent awakening,
each glimpse of the divine.

Reunion

It was summer
and the bright, reaffirming waves
rolled down across everything,
coursing through our limbs,
bringing out the warm, languid affection
in which movement and laughter
flowed freely between us.

It is summer again today
and we, reunited,
don't need to work to make connection —
It's here
in the liquid lines that join us
deeper than words,
deeper than roles,
deeper than thought.

The rhythm of summer

Everything is moving in the rhythm
of summer —
sound of wind chimes,
scent of privet,
transfixing flit of
not-quite-random insects,
play of light on spider webs,
crows in conversation —

There is something to learn from this,
something to take with me
from the unhurried connection of events,
the space between
that's long enough for slack,
supple so it ripples smoothly.

Here where it's too hot
for spiking urgency
or any worry,
things still progress
prodigiously,
with ample room
to take their perfect time.

Daily Poems

Every day has a poem in it —
That little girl starting to run,
short-stringed kite two feet above her head,
Her mom, walking behind her, smiling
(colors: pink, purple, red)
That man on racing bike,
his smile denoting deep contentment —
Each of these are poems
though only briefly intersected here

Clouds dance along horizon
reminding me there's more
than the smell of tar,
the roar of motors;
There are
Echo tunnels on the trail,
A chalk-drawn paean to Love
(now almost washed away)
And a delighted Downs boy with a dog.
The sun begins to cook the day under the overcast.
The coolness sighs and looks for places to lie down.
The wind bears thistle fluff along
and sets it in the river,
Small girls with their grandma play around.

Every day has a poem in it —
I only need to dip my head in
like these ducks,
Reach beneath the surface,
Pull it up.

IV. Prayer
— Comfort and healing

Holding On

Take me in
to hidden chambers,
Lift the secret latches,
Solve the puzzle locks,
Bring me into mystery
and endow me there.
What I've heard in silence
I will shout from mountains —
It is right
that everybody hear this truth,
That it begin to offer
another way of seeing,
another way to be:

        Spirit, I will hold you.
        I will cling
        like an infant
        to my mother —
        I will not let go,
        I'll feel the flow
        of infant love
        that holds on tight with such need
        in the instinct of connection
        but not in desperation —
        in affection

Spirit, when we fly
and the wind rushes around us
and the land
falls away beneath us
and the air grows cool,
I will cling
to your warmth,
I will hold on with love
and whoop
with heart-rush joy.

In this house of prayer

In this house of prayer
that is me —
everything I am —
With daily intermittent bursts
I find
the freedom from all other law.

No weight of history,
no drag of social norms,
no march of time,
no fear, no fading sense,
no falling off of purpose,
no decay
can touch the being
I am learning here.

Surrendered to the dawn of the divine,
my every move impelled
by that which constantly
surprises me,
I find its grace, its elegance —
so intricate, so fine —
unfolds my joy to feel
the Soul-force that comprises me.

In this house of prayer
I learn to move in love,
to see that this is what I am
and all I live to prove.

a humble prayer

today
let me own no opinion
let me be led
let me not try
to construct meaning,
envision purpose,
steer my craft.
there is plenty here
in this receptive place,
enough to do
in learning, listening, following
that I don't need
to pull a plan from the air,
don't need to
invent or vaunt myself —
it's enough
to be here.

One Thing

The things I don't understand
are myriad.
I forget that, sometimes.
I forget it when I'm flying,
When I'm swooping,
When I'm surfing on the joy of life.

It's when I find myself in the morass,
Churning, flailing,
That all my simple answers seem
like the fur of a dowsed cat —
Exposing scrawny neck and bony frame,
No longer capable of warming,
Void of the buoyancy required
to lift me out.

But then
Whenever did my flight
rely on my own knowledge?
Maybe it doesn't matter
what I don't understand —
Maybe I only need to know
One thing.

Love's Plan

I'm not allowed to think myself alone
and struggling to find where I belong —
Each effort to invent myself will fall
as sure as piles of sand against the sea.
So it is with things I haven't done,
and times I've been so proud, and been so wrong —
There never was a chance for them at all
as long as I had hopes to rescue me.
A precious part of Love's unique design
is how the loss of what I have called mine
will reset my assumptions, so I find
identity at one with the divine.
So, meekly cleansed, I then can lift my face
to Love's bright pattern and my perfect place.

Pool of Bethesda

No angel at a certain season
guards the gate to wholeness.
You don't have to wait
until the water stirs,
nor can the others
clambering before you
deprive you of your right
to stand up free.

Truth needs no conduit, no channel,
no narrow source to shine its light —
It pours forth spherical, eternal,
Its reign established, sovereign and bright.

(It has been said
To know the truth shall make you free.
If this is true
It means that free is what you are
and isn't something needing to be given,
nor something you're approaching from afar)

It is the same with love
(Please let my life be one that shows it)
No angel, bright or dark, can claim
it stands there to deliver or withhold it.
No one can fail, right now,
To be the miracle someone has ever sought,
nor fail to see that they are loved
and so bestowed the peace that passes thought.

Learning to Heal

I feel the power of Truth; its touch excites
and ripples in the torch my heart ignites.
I love how I'm alive, but I want more —
I want to exercise Truth's healing power.
This fact I know: I need to live consistent —
In this, Truth is imperative, insistent.
What Soul impels must follow through as Soul —
No other cause or god renders me whole.
Just as it's true that if I really love,
my love unbinds me, sends euphoria
concatenating down through each encounter,
to make my store of joy into a mountain.
I can't go harboring the phantom fear
if I want perfect healing to come clear.

Healing

Love flows in
to all the hidden places —
Love's balm,
Love's calm
allays all fear, aligns the inner graces.
Every anxious flailing churning clamoring
is put to rest in Love's deep-running channeling.
Only what is wholesome can grow here,
All progress so attuned to Love,
all purpose clear.
Let me humbly move at Love's direction,
Hallowed in Love's joy and pure affection,
So removed from every claim of pain,
Firm and settled in Love's holy reign.

Lullaby for Heather

Mother Love, wrap up your child
in comprehensive arms,
Broad enough to hold her every hope,
Soft enough to nurture all her charms,
Close enough to smooth her brow
and rest her eyes,
Strong enough to bear her
swiftly through the dreaming skies.
Synchronize her heart with yours,
Refresh her with your peace,
Deliver her with clarity,
and new found ease.
Mother Love, infuse her with
your bright delight
and bold and brilliant action
in the morning light.

Lullaby for Edward

Spirit current, take this man,
Move as him in light and sound,
Bear him on a journey of remembering.

Fill the hollow of his soul,
Let him know himself as whole,
Coursing joy and steady strength engendering.

All that he has been since long before the dawn of time
Let it flow through him in a reverberating chime
Bring him through the shadow of these weary days
Fill his heart with laughter and his lips with praise
Let him fly in surety that everywhere he's roamed
He's always been in your embrace
And so forever home.

Bedtime Prayer

One last cocooning prayer
before I sleep,
One last tuning
with that which keeps me,
One last recall
of what prevents my fall —
The tender cradle
that enwraps us all

The cozy blankets
and the horizontal plane
won't, on their own
assure my peace
but my true thanks
and prayer with soft refrain
will bring me home
and set my soul at ease.

Shared Prayer, King County Jail

After we finished talking
(in patchwork mix of four imperfect languages)
She held my gaze
and held it
till it became a carrier wave,
and lacking words,
I let myself sink into prayer.
I sent it out across the visual tone,
I found the place
where we are one,
I found the power
present in the infinite,
the source we share
that nothing can assail.
She nodded understanding
as if I had been speaking.
("Estoy orando" I said then;
"I am understanding," she replied)
and we did another round,
silent, deeper
till I felt myself changed
in the broad terrain
where we found ourselves —
knew that this was somewhere
far more solid than the stories of our lives.
"I hope," she said, in Portuspanish,
"someday I can do for someone
what you have done for me."
"I'm sure," I said in Spanish,
"that you will."

Prayer at the End of Days

Spirit, be a rock under my feet,
For these sands are flowing hard against me.
Hold me with your steady hand,
Unite me with your center,
Give me strength to stand
Against the seething flood of matter.
Be so clear
That all these tidal flows
Will fail to grab me in their undertow.
Let them only serve to bring illusion down
That I may stand in freedom
Knowing Truth alone.
Hold us all, that as the turbid turbulence subsides,
We all will stand together
Seeing new, clear-eyed.

Arcturus and his sons

There's no gap
Between what I want
and what I'm given,
Between what I need
and present heaven

There's no desire
that would conspire
to turn me from my truth,
For truth and my desire are ever one

There's no part of me
that's separate from who I am,
No part that needs to be expunged or changed,
The Principle in which I am designed
remains the same,
Holding my life, like all the stars
exquisitely arranged.

Light's drawing

Light draws me
I do not draw myself
These dark and awkward pencil jabs
don't capture who I am

Light glides across,
Illumines me
from any angle one might view.
The lines I make are stuck upon a page —
They can't move with the day
so can't be true

Light, draw me
clearly towards yourself,
Be my life, my day, my song.
I cast my foolish pencil down
to shine with you
where I belong.

Another prayer of thanks

Thank you, Life, for showing me
what it is to love,
To feel that bright, igniting joy
at someone's presence in my days
And with each flash of love
be brought to life

Thank you, Life, for showing me
what it is to be loved,
To feel that luminescent circle
holding me
Embracing me in tender, warming glow

Thank you for the shimmer of awareness
that I can always love
and reap the richness of that blessing
all the time

Thank you for the sureness
that I am always loved
And I can rest there
Everywhere at home.

Praying in the dark

Spirit, light, today I need
some warming core,
some inner seed
some steady, peaceful, self-contained assurance
that all is well within, that my endurance
won't even be stretched thin by these dark days,
that that which rises up within to sing your praise
will carry me in joy along whatever course you choose,
will bubble forth and grow more strong
the more it's used,
so glowing with a warmth
that I can feel and also share,
thus showing forth your presence
here and everywhere.

Cradling Prayer

Arms of Love
I see
how your hold on me
and on this house
so gently cradles us
and so allows
the meek and sweet emergence
of every heart's desire
and each extending outward
of what we glimpse we are,
Which, with the simple screen of your attention
You nourish and augment,
While all our grinding efforts
and the fears and thoughts that block us
simply fall away into the void

And in your arms
we glow, we shine,
Safe in this hallowed place,
we snuggle in
and then reach out
resplendent in your grace.

Prayer for myself

Fear not, little one —
You aren't responsible
for imaging yourself.
It's not your thoughts
that make you ill,
It's not your thoughts
that make you whole,
It's not that you must find
some secret button to control
the things you feel and manifest today.

The Love that heals you
is its own bright, steady source —
It reveals you
and sets you on your course,
And you can feel
its tender, cleansing touch.
You'll know it's real,
You'll know it is enough.
Fear not, for every cell of you is held
in perfect calm,
serenely peaceful, well.

Guidance Prayer

Today, Spirit, I entrust
all my thoughts to you
because I must —
I know the courses I have run
have many sinkholes, many ruts,
And if I set out on my own,
their deep-worn tracks
will ever thrust me
down the same false paths again

Spirit, today I float
with your calm breath to guide me.
Hold my quiet hope
a growing light inside me.
Let your wisdom cope
with every maze my thought may chase,
Let me fly with you —
Impart your grace.
Wean me of those old recursions,
Make me new,
Let me be your mirror, through and through.
Let me grasp, in this and every minute,
your vast and shining world
and my place in it.

A Moment

For an instant,
in my prayer,
I saw all the darkness of the world
as being short as a breath —
an exhale awaiting the inhale,
an infant's need reaching out
to be gathered into loving mother arms,
And all the world's travails,
throughout all time,
as just that moment of the asking,
calling forth the full embrace
that brings us all in and in.

Peace Channel

Let me move in the peace channel
Defined and defended by thought
Where no worry can dart in
No recurring pitches
about what is wrong
and how someone else
should fix it
No stress about my best chance
and how I might miss it
No harping on mistakes
and dour predictions

Let the peace channel run strong
in the clarity
of my knowing
Nothing mars the calm song
of my being
or the perfect place
for everyone
to move in broad and tranquil ease
as Mind's bright conceiving,
now and all along,
of everything that is.

Vision Prayer

Spirit, today
You can have my eyes —
Hold them holy,
Guide the light they gather,
Give them focus.
Let them synthesize
the clear truth you display,
Let them harmonize
the elements of your day,
Let me empathize
with everyone I see
So that I understand
your comprehensive ownership of me,
The way your grace illumines
everything I know,
all that I am.

"In my Father's house"

In this house
There's room enough for everyone.
There's room for those
who need to go slow,
whose moves are ponderous
and often hesitating,
Who may seem to forget sometimes
where they are going.

There's room for those
who only lightly touch down
in the quick flitting of skittering motion,
Hardly here for long enough
to cast a shadow,
But wanting to have weight
and be remembered.

There's room for those who need to lead
And those who wish to follow,
Room to blaze in brilliance,
Room to wait in silence.
Room for both those born within
And those who came from far,
Room for all to grow
and so step in to what they are.

Fundamental frequency

Let me sink
into this hammock,
This cocoon,
This softly swaying place
Where my weight is cradled
by the kindness
of the force that holds me here

Let me swing
in the fundamental frequency
of that which breathes the cosmos,
Singing me
as it sings the stars —
Lullaby of motion

Let me fall
gently to my center
where the quiet pulsing hope
remains connected
to the universal light
and hums the harmony
of that great song
that carries me in sweetness
through the night.

Steadying

Spirit, your eye
knows how to appraise me
You know how
to cradle my head in your hands
and tenderly reset
each strand of hair
each ruffled thought
each foolish misconception

You know how to set me steady
Hold me till my inner balance
finds itself
Send me on my course so gently
I can feel the poise to guide myself

Spirit, your gaze
is so clear
When I see with your eyes
I know that what I see is true:
My love is strong, my joy is pure —
I choose your sight
to see through,
I choose your sight
to see me through.

Companioned Prayer

Let me take you with me
on a prayer
Where we first plunge
into the wonder of our source —
The nature and the nurture of
the law that holds us
pouring forth the affluence of Life
Then in the insistent,
naturally occurring
alignment of our systems
with what always is,
we'll feel the surging strengthening,
the calm and gentle ordering,
the unrestrained empowering
of everything we are —
Our hope, our worth, our destiny,
Our interwoven harmony,
The easy, brilliant artistry
written in the book of us
long before the birthing
of the stars.

The Light of Truth

Here in the still quiet
I can't hold myself down too long
For all around me
Light rises
Like steady bubbles from underwater
Like steam from morning lakes

And no darkness can be amassed
to stop it
And no denial can distract me
from the fact that it is here —
Not a construct of my thinking,
Nothing I, through will or thought,
can fail to see

The light is here
The only true fact of being —
In all honesty
the only thing
we ever truly know.

About these poems

All but two of these poems were written as part of a discipline I established at the beginning of 2011 — to write a poem a day. Though my first efforts were mostly concerned with form, meter, and rhyme, I soon discovered that the main purpose of this practice, for me, was to focus on and capture the life impression, for that day, of my most salient truth. On some days it is a simple appreciation of the weather and the life forces it illustrates; on other days there's some philosophical or spiritual epiphany that I need to record. The four collections gathered in this volume all share some sense of journeying, though more in the life-quest sense than in the sense of physical travel. The first set, *Journeying*, is about life questing in particular. The second set, *Thought's Landscapes*, explores philosophical questions around such themes as story and time. The third set, *Earth Whispers*, is a tribute to weather and seasons. The fourth set, *Prayer*, may represent my most frequent direction for journeying. All of these poems have appeared on my blog, wendymulhernpoetry.blogspot.com, where you can also find each of my daily poems.

— *Wendy Mulhern, 2013*

About the author

Wendy Mulhern is a poet, a spiritual seeker, a dancer. She lives in Seattle with her husband, her father-in-law, and her two almost grown children, when they are not away at school. She writes a poem a day (almost) and publishes her poems at wendymulhernpoetry.blogspot.com. For news of her print publications, see wendymulhern.com.

Also by Wendy Mulhern:

Revolution — *poems of the necessary uprising*

Revolution is a call to action — not so much the dogged plodding of political activism as the rising of hearts in the spontaneous assertion of the right to live full and free. Wendy Mulhern's poems offer inspiration and empowerment, and her artwork unfolds a story of strength and hope.

Capture Rapture —*notes from the romance adventure.*

Capture Rapture is about romance — all facets of it — from the initial attraction through all the uncertainties and questions, and including both the joy of union and the necessary regrouping when things don't work out as hoped. Through all the aspects of romance, it provides spiritual resources that lead to the calm of love.

Cuddle your Curmudgeons —*domestic storms and sunbreaks*

Cuddle your Curmudgeons is a tender and honest look at the heartaches and joys of family life. These poems are the most personal and particular ones the author has written, covering a short period when her children are teenagers, and the family members struggle for harmony, connection, and a clear sense of purpose. Through the struggles shine bright gleams of the triumph of love and the victory of peace in her household.

wendymulhern.com
wendymulhernpoetry.blogspot.com